Fact Finders®

First-Person Histories

DIARY OF
SALLY WISTER
A
COLONIAL QUAKER GIRL

by Sally Wister

CAPSTONE PRESS
a capstone imprint

Fact Finders Books are published by Capstone Press,
1710 Roe Crest Drive, North Mankato, Minnesota 56003
www.capstonepub.com

Library of Congress Cataloging-in-Publication Data
Cataloging-in-publication information is on file with the Library of Congress.
ISBN 978-1-4765-4191-4 (library binding)
ISBN 978-1-4765-5134-0 (paperback)
ISBN 978-1-4765-5983-4 (eBook PDF)

Editorial Credits
Michelle Hasselius, editor; Bobbie Nuytten, designer; Wanda Winch, media researcher; Laura Manthe, production specialist

Photo Credits
The Bridgeman Art Library: Valley Forge Historical Society, USA, 12 (bottom); Capstone 19; Collection of the Maryland State Archives, Artist: Charles Willson Peale (1741-1827), Title: William Smallwood (1732-1792), Date: 1823, Medium: Oil on canvas, Dimensions: 29 x 24", Accession no.: MSA SC 1545-1054, 14; Dress photo courtesy of Matti's Millinery and Costumes. Hair, make-up and gown courtesy of Matti's Millinery & Costumes of www.mattionline.com, 24; http://www.jamesmannartfarm.com/jmas16.html, 7; iStockphoto Inc.: Nic_Taylor, cover, 23 (flag); James P. Rowan, 21; Library of Congress: Prints and Photographs Division, 9, 18, 20, 28 (bottom); National Parks Service: Colonial National Historical Park, 26, Keith Rocco, artist, cover, 1 (right); National Parks Service: Harpers Ferry Center/Keith Rocco, artist, 29; North Wind Picture Archives, 5, 11, 15, 17, 25; Shutterstock/Andrzej Sowa, cover (vintage setting left), Katya Ulitina, cover (background), Mike Flippo, 28 (top), Picksfive, ripped paper design, Veronika Kachalkina, 12 (top); SuperStock Inc.: SuperStock, 22; Wikipedia, 8

Printed in the United States of America in Stevens Point, Wisconsin.
092013   007769WZS14

TABLE OF
CONTENTS

A
Colonial Quaker Girl

In 1777 war forced Sally Wister and her family to leave their home in Philadelphia, Pennsylvania. Pennsylvania and 12 other American colonies were fighting the Revolutionary War (1775–1783) for their independence from Great Britain. The British troops had defeated the colonies' Continental Army in Pennsylvania and were about to capture Philadelphia.

Before the British troops entered the city, Sally and her family escaped to North Wales, Pennsylvania. The Wisters stayed with Sally's aunt, Hannah Foulke, a widow with three children.

Sally, who's full name was Sarah, and her family were **Quakers**. Quakers are pacifists. They do not believe in fighting or in war. Because of this belief, many colonists thought Quakers were British sympathizers, or **Tories**. But Sally's diary implies that her family was sympathetic to the American cause.

As a daughter of a prominent Quaker family, Sally was well-educated. She attended "dame school" where she learned reading, writing, arithmetic, and needlework. Most girls her age did not receive such a good education in the late 1770s.

Sally was around 16 years old when she wrote her diary, telling what life was like during the Revolutionary War. This Quaker family, because of their wealth and religion, was more removed from the pain and death of war than other colonists. But Sally's diary helps us understand how frightening it was to live in the midst of soldiers, guns, and cannon fire. Her diary also gives us an idea of what life was like in colonial America.

In this painting from the 1700s, colonists walk by Independence Hall in Philadelphia in 1776.

Quaker—a member of the Religious Society of Friends, a group founded in the 1600s, that prefers simple religious services and opposes war

Tory—an American sympathetic to the British army

5

THE Diary OF Sally Wister
1777–1778

September 25, 1777—

To <u>*Deborah Norris*</u>*:*

Tho' I have not the least shadow of an opportunity to send a letter, if I do write, I will keep a sort of journal of the time that may expire before I see thee ...

Yesterday ... two Virginia officers call'd our house, and inform'd us that the British Army has cross'd the Schuylkill [River]. Presently after, another person stopp'd, and confirm'd ... that Gen'l Washington and Army were near Pottsgrove. Well, thee may be sure we were sufficiently scared; however, the road was very still till evening.

About seven o'clock we heard a great noise. To the door we all went. A large number of waggons, with about three hundred of the Philadelphia **Militia**. They begged for drink, and several push'd into the house. One of those that entered was a little tipsy, and had a mind to be saucy.

Sally's diary entries appear word for word as they were written, whenever possible. Because the diary appears in its original form, you will notice misspellings and mistakes in grammar. To make Sally's meaning clear, in some instances, corrections or explanations within a set of brackets sometimes follow the mistakes. Sometimes text has been removed from the diary entries. In these cases, you will notice three dots in a row, which are called ellipses. Ellipses show that words or sentences are missing from the text.

I then thought it time for me to retreat; so figure me (mightily scar'd, as not having presence of mind enough to face so many of the Military), running in at one door, and out another, all in a shake with fear; but after a while, seeing the officers appear gentlemanly, and the soldiers civil, I call'd reason to my aid. My fears were in some measure dispell'd tho' my teeth rattled, and my hand shook like an aspen leaf. They did not offer to take their quarters with us; so with many blessings, and as many **adieus**, they marched off. I have given thee the most material occurrences of yesterday faithfully.

Sally wrote her diary as a letter to her cousin Deborah Norris. The two girls were reunited after the war, when Deborah most likely read about Sally's adventures.

The Liberty Bell was moved from Philadelphia before British troops took control of the city in 1777, as shown in this 1976 mural from Quakertown, Pennsylvania.

militia—an army composed of ordinary citizens
adieu—the French word for good-bye

7

September 25—

This day, till twelve o'clock, the road was mighty quiet, when Hobson Jones came riding along ... and said the British were at Skippack road; that we should soon see their **light horse**, and [that] a party of **Hessians** had actually turn'd into our lane. My Dadda and Mamma gave it the credit it deserv'd, for he does not keep strictly to the truth in all respects; but the delicate, chicken-hearted Liddy and I were wretchedly scar'd. We cou'd say nothing but "Oh! what shall we do? What will become of us?" These questions only augmented the terror we were in.

Well, the fright went off. We saw no light horse or Hessians. O. Foulke came here in the evening, and told us that Gen'l Washington had come down as far as the Trappe [River] ...

The British hired Hessian soldiers, shown in this 1799 illustration on night patrol, to fight the colonists in the Revolutionary War.

In this painting from 1912, General George Washington and his troops cross the Delaware River to surprise Hessian soldiers in 1776.

Moster.
1912.

Defeating the Hessians

The Hessians were German soldiers paid by the British to fight the colonists. The presence of these soldiers made the colonists angry. The colonists saw the war as being only between them and the British.

The Hessians earned their living by hiring themselves out as soldiers. They fought in battles throughout Europe. There they had a reputation as brutal fighters. The Hessians also stole from peoples' homes.

During the Revolutionary War, soldiers did not fight in the winter. But the Continental Army General George Washington saw that the American cause was desperate. In December 1776 he organized a surprise attack on a group of Hessian soldiers. The Hessians were camped in Trenton, New Jersey. Washington led his troops by boat across the partially frozen Delaware River. The troops surprised the sleepy Hessians and defeated them.

light horse—a soldier who rode on a horse that weighed less than a draft horse

Hessian—a German soldier paid by the British to fight the colonists

September 26—

... I was standing in the kitchen about 12, when somebody came to me in a hurry, screaming, "Sally, Sally, here are the light horse!" This was by far the greatest fright I had endured; fear tack'd wings to my feet; I was at the house in a moment; at the porch I stopt, and it really was the light horse.

I ran immediately to the western door, where the family were assembled, anxiously waiting for the event. They rode up to the door and halted, and enquired if we had horses to sell; he was answer'd negatively.

"Have not you, sir," to my father, "two black horses?"

"Yes, but I have no mind to dispose of them."

My terror had by this time nearly subsided. The officer and the men behav'd perfectly civil; the first drank two glasses of wine, rode away, bidding his men follow, which, after adieus in number, they did ...

It has rained all afternoon, and to present appearances, will all night. In all probability the English will take possession of the city to-morrow or next day. What a change will it be! May the Almighty take you under His protection, for without His divine aid all human assistance is vain ...

The uncertainty of our position engrosses me quite. Perhaps to be in the midst of war, and ruin, and the clang of arms. But we must hope for the best ...

> By 1775 Philadelphia was the largest city in the American colonies. More than 250,000 people lived there. The city became the colonial capital in 1790.

Quakers worship informally in meeting houses, as shown in this illustration of a colonial Quaker spinning yarn while worshipping.

The Quaker Religion

Quakers, also known as the Religious Society of Friends, are Christians who believe that God lives in every person's mind. Quakers call this a person's "inner" or "inward light." Quakers' beliefs are known as testimonies. These testimonies are peace, honesty, and simplicity.

Quakers worship informally in meeting houses. A meeting house is a plain building. There are no decorations or music in a meeting house. Quakers believe these customs interfere with the practice of talking to God.

Quakers oppose military violence of any kind. Quakers in the colonies often faced fines or jail terms for refusing to join armies or pay taxes to help improve military forts. Many communities offered Quakers alternatives to serving in armies. They allowed Quakers to hire substitutes or pay fees. But many Quakers believed these options still supported violence.

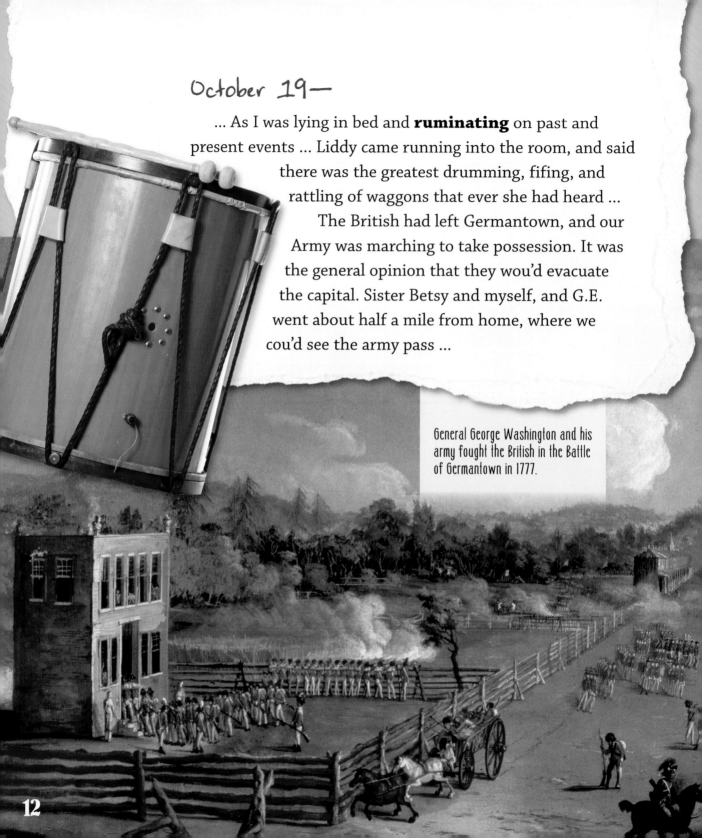

October 19—

... As I was lying in bed and **ruminating** on past and present events ... Liddy came running into the room, and said there was the greatest drumming, fifing, and rattling of waggons that ever she had heard ...

The British had left Germantown, and our Army was marching to take possession. It was the general opinion that they wou'd evacuate the capital. Sister Betsy and myself, and G.E. went about half a mile from home, where we cou'd see the army pass ...

General George Washington and his army fought the British in the Battle of Germantown in 1777.

12

Most Quakers lived a simple life and wore plain clothes. But the Wisters were wealthy and wore fashionable clothes. Sally often describes in her diary the fancy, colorful dresses she wore.

Several officers call'd to get some refreshment, but none of consequence till the afternoon. Cousin Prissa and myself were sitting at the door; I in a green skirt, dark short gown ... Two genteel men of the military order rode up to the door: "Your servant, ladies," ... ask'd if they cou'd have quarters for Genl. Smallwood. Aunt Foulke thought she cou'd accommodate them ...

In the evening his Generalship came with six attendants, which compos'd his family, a large guard of soldiers, a number of horses and baggage-waggons. The yard and house were in confusion, and glitter'd with military equipments ...

How new is our situation! I feel good in spirits, though surrounded by an Army, the house is full of officers, the yard alive with soldiers,—very peaceable sort of men, tho'. They eat like other folks, talk like them, and behave themselves with elegance; so I will not be afraid of them ...

ruminate—to think deeply about something

October 20—

... The General is tall, portly, well made: a truly **martial** air, the behaviour and manner of a gentleman, a good understanding, & great humanity of **disposition**, constitute the character of Smallwood ...

Well, here comes the glory, the Major, so bashful, so famous ... I at first thought the Major cross and proud, but I was mistaken. He is about nineteen, nephew to the Gen'l, and acts as Major of **brigade** to him; he cannot be extoll'd for the graces of person, but for those of the mind he may justly be celebrated ...

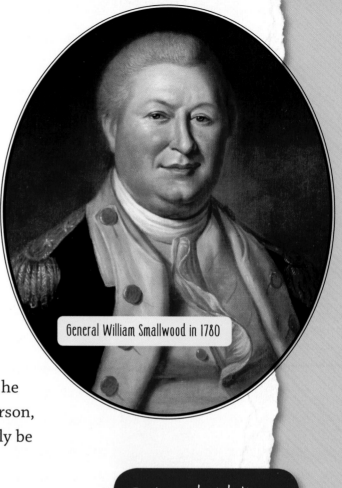

General William Smallwood in 1780

October 27—

We had again the pleasure of the Gen'l ... at afternoon tea. He (the Gen'l, I mean) is most agreeable; so lively, so free, and chats so gaily ... The Major and I had a little chat to ourselves this eve. No harm, I assure thee: he and I are friends.

During colonial times people gathered twice each day for tea time. Families invited friends and neighbors to tea to exchange the news of the day.

Colonists in the 1700s served tea as a way to socialize with family and friends.

November 1—

To-day the Militia marches, and the Gen'l and officers leave us. Heigh ho! I am very sorry; for when you have been with agreeable people, 'tis impossible not to feel regret when they bid you adieu, perhaps forever ...

martial—warlike and fierce

disposition—a person's general attitude or temperament

brigade—a unit of an army, usually made up of two or more battalions

December 6, 4 o'clock—

I was much alarm'd just now, sitting in the parlour [**parlor**] ... when somebody burst open the door, "Sally, here's Major Stodard!"

I jumped. Our **conjectures** were various concerning his coming. The poor fellow, from great fatigue and want of rest, together with being expos'd to the night air, had caught cold, which brought on a fever. He cou'd scarcely walk, and I went into aunt's to see him.

I was surpris'd. Instead of the lively, alert, blooming Stodard, who was on his feet the instant we enter'd, he look'd pale, thin, and dejected, too weak to rise. A bow, and "How are you, miss Sally?"

"How does thee do, Major?"

I seated myself near him, inquir'd the cause of his indisposition, ask'd for the Gen'l, reciev'd his compliments. Not willing to fatigue him with too much chat, I bid him adieu.

To-night Aunt Hanna Foulke ... administer'd something. Jesse assisted him to his **chamber**. He had not lain down five minutes before he was fast asleep. Adieu. I hope we shall enjoy a good night's rest.

December 11—

Our Army mov'd, as we thought, to go into winter **quarters**, but we hear there is a party of the enemy gone over Schuylkill; so our Army went to look at them.

I observ'd to Stodard, "So you are going to leave us to the English."

"Yes, ha! ha! ha! leave you for the English."

parlor—a formal living room

conjecture—a conclusion you reach by guessing

chamber—a bedroom

quarters—housing used by the military

George Washington selected Valley Forge because of its high ground and position near the Schuylkill River. He lead his troops to winter camp in December 1777.

He has a certain indifference about him sometimes that to strangers is not very pleasing. He sometimes is silent for minutes. One of these silent fits was interrupted the other day by his clasping his hands and exclaiming aloud, "Oh, my God, I wish this war was at an end!"

December 19—

The officers, after the politest adieus, have left us ... I feel sorry at their departure, yet 'tis a different kind from what I felt some time since ...

December 20—

General Washington's army have gone into winter quarters at the Valley Forge. We shall not see many of the military now. We shall be very intimate with **solitude** ...

George Washington's army tried to make shelters before the snow fell at Valley Forge in 1777.

solitude—being alone

Cruel Winter at Valley Forge

In October 1777 General Washington's 11,000 soldiers set up camp at Valley Forge. Soldiers tried to build small huts before the cold and snow reached the Pennsylvania countryside. But winter came early. By December most soldiers still lived in tents.

Shipping food and supplies to Valley Forge was difficult. The British controlled Philadelphia and did not allow wagons to transport food from distant markets. Soon, supplies were scarce.

The soldiers' clothing and shoes were worn out. Many had only rags to cover their frozen feet.

The Colonial government did not have enough money to buy food and other goods. The government printed paper money, but its value decreased as the war continued. For this reason, many American farmers and merchants stopped selling supplies to the Continental Army. Continental soldiers viewed this as a betrayal by their own country.

This illustration shows the bitterly cold winter Washington's army suffered through at Valley Forge.

May 11, 1778—

The scarcity of paper, which is very great in this part of the country, and the three last months producing hardly anything material, has prevented me from keeping a regular account of things; but to-day the scene begins to brighten, and I will continue my non-sense.

In the afternoon, we were just seated at tea ... Nelly ... brought us the wonderful intelligence that there were light horse in the road. The tea-table was almost deserted. About 15 light horse were the **vanguard** of 16 hundred men under the command of Gen'l Maxwell. I imagin'd that they wou'd pass immediately by, but I was agreeably disappointed. My father came in with the Gen'l, Col. Broadhead, Major Ogden and Capt. Jones ...

American soldiers marched through towns like Sally's on their way to battle, shown in this drawing from around 1881.

vanguard—the leading or foremost position of any army advancing into battle

May [15 or 29], evening—

This afternoon has been productive of adventures in the true sense of the word. Jenny Roberts, Betsy, Liddy, and I, very genteelly dress'd, determined to take a stroll. Neighbor Morgan's was proposed and agreed to. Away we rambled, heedless girls. Pass'd two picket guards. Meeting with no interruptions encourag'd us.

After paying our visit, we walked towards home, when, to my utter astonishment, the **sentry** desir'd us to stop; that he had orders not to suffer any persons to pass but those who had leave from the officer, who was at the guard house, surrounded by a number of men. To go to him would be inconsistent with propriety; to stay there, and night advancing, was not clever.

I was much terrified. I try'd to persuade the soldier to let us pass. "No; he dared not." Betsy attempted to go. He presented his gun, with the bayonet fix'd. This was an additional fright.

Back we turn'd; and, very fortunately, the officer Capt. Emeson [Emerson], seeing our distress, came to us. I ask'd him if he had any objection to our passing the sentry. "None at all, ma'am." He waited upon us, and reprimanded the man, and we, without any further difficulty, came home.

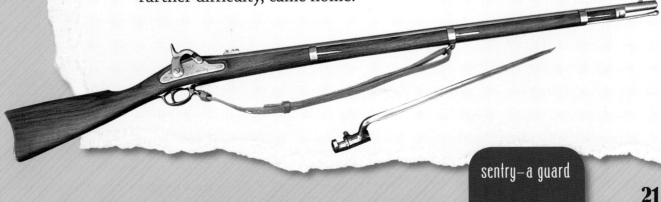

sentry—a guard

June 3—

... A horseman deliver'd this message: "Let the troop lie on their arms, and be ready to march at a moment's warning."

He immediately gave those orders to the sergeant. Every soldier was in motion. I was a good deal frighten'd, and ask'd Watts the reason. He fancy'd the British were in motion, tho' he had not receiv'd such intelligence.

Many British troops destroyed colonial homes during the Revolutionary War, as shown in this painting from the 1800s.

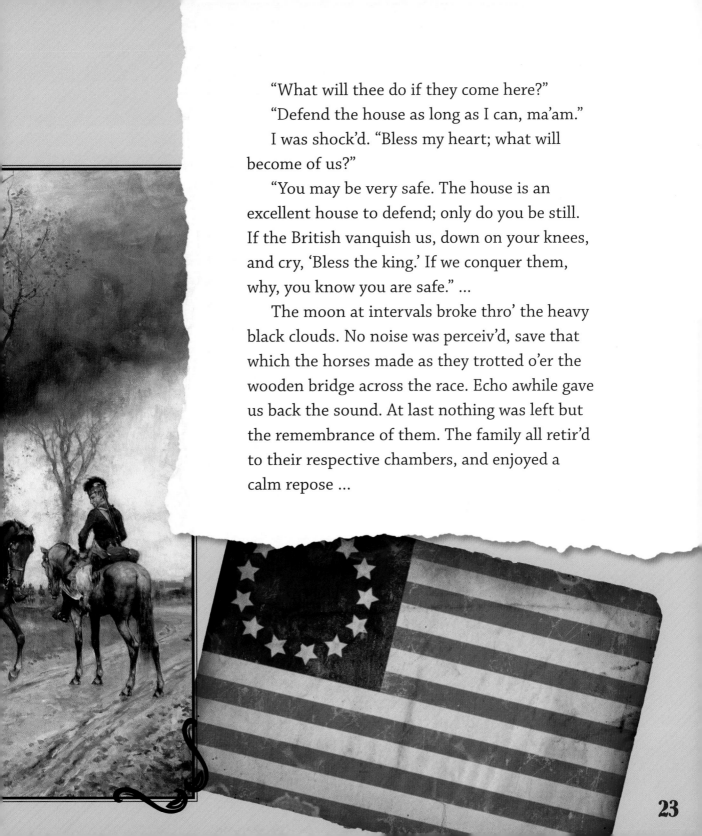

"What will thee do if they come here?"

"Defend the house as long as I can, ma'am."

I was shock'd. "Bless my heart; what will become of us?"

"You may be very safe. The house is an excellent house to defend; only do you be still. If the British vanquish us, down on your knees, and cry, 'Bless the king.' If we conquer them, why, you know you are safe." …

The moon at intervals broke thro' the heavy black clouds. No noise was perceiv'd, save that which the horses made as they trotted o'er the wooden bridge across the race. Echo awhile gave us back the sound. At last nothing was left but the remembrance of them. The family all retir'd to their respective chambers, and enjoyed a calm repose …

June 5—

Last night we were a little alarm'd. I was awaken'd about 12 o'clock with somebody's opening the chamber door. I observ'd Cousin Prissa talking to Mamma. I asked what was the matter.

"Only a party of light horse."

"Are they Americans?" I quickly said.

She answer'd in the affirmative (which dispell'd my fears) ... this morn I rose by or near seven, dress'd in my light chintz, which is made gown-fashion, kenting handkerchief, and linen apron.

"Sufficiently smart for a country girl, Sally."

Don't call me a country girl, Debby Norris. Please to observe that I pride myself upon being a Philadelphian, and that a residence of 20 months has not at all diminished the love I have for that dear place; and as soon as one very capital alteration takes place (which is very much talk'd of at present), I expect to return to it with a double pleasure.

an example of a colonial dress worn between the 1760s and 1770s

June 18—

Rose at half-past four this morning. Iron'd industriously til one o'clock, din'd [dined], went up stairs, threw myself on the bed, and fell asleep. About four sister Hannah waked me, and said uncle and Foulke were down stairs; so I decorated myself, and went down. Felt quite **lackadaisical** … We have had strange reports about the British being about leaving Philada …

This illustration from 1800 shows homes on Market Street in Philadelphia, where the Wister family moved back to after the war.

lackadaisical—lazy

June 19—

We have heard an astonishing piece of news! – that the English have entirely left the city! It is almost impossible! Stay, I shall hear further.

Although the British left Philadelphia in 1778, the war continued. This illustration shows Washington's headquarters for the Battle of Yorktown.

June 19, Evening—

A light horseman has just confirm'd the above intelligence! This is **charmante**! They decamp'd yesterday. He (the horseman) was in Philada. It is true. They have gone. Past a doubt. I can't help forbear exclaiming to the girls,—

"Now are you sure the news is true? Now are you sure they have gone?"

"Yes, yes, yes!" they all cry, "and may they never, never return." ...

June 20—

... Our brave, our heroic General Washington was escorted by fifty of the Life Guard, with drawn swords. Each day he acquires an addition to his goodness ...

So shall now conclude this journal with humbly hoping that the Great Disposer of events, who has graciously **vouchsaf'd** to protect us to this day through many dangers, will still be pleas'd to continue his protection.

The Life Guard was a unit of the army created to protect General George Washington during the Revolutionary War.

charmante—charming

vouchsafe—to grant something in a gracious manner

Life in Philadelphia

After Sally's family returned to Philadelphia, she lived the rest of her life in the family's home on Market Street. Sally became a quiet, religious woman. Like all deeply religious Quakers, she avoided novels and the theater and advised her friends to do likewise. She read religious works, wrote poetry, did good deeds, and cared for her sick mother. She died only months after her mother in 1804 at the age of 43.

Timeline

- Dates in Sally Wister's life
- Important dates in the Revolutionary War

1776

The Declaration of Independence is signed in Philadelphia.

1761

Sally is born in Philadelphia.

1776

General Washington's army crosses the Delaware River to surprise and defeat the Hessian army in Trenton, New Jersey.

1760 — **1776**

1778

The Wisters move back to Philadelphia after British troops leave the city.

1804

Sally dies in Philadelphia at the age of 43.

1783

The Treaty of Paris officially ends the Revolutionary War.

1777-1778

Washington's army camps at Valley Forge without enough supplies for the harsh winter conditions.

1781

The armies of General Washington, the Marquis de Lafayette, and General Jean Rochambeau defeat the British in the Battle of Yorktown.

1777

The Wisters begin to quarter Continental Army officers.

1777

The Continental Army defeats the British in the Battle of Saratoga, New York.

1777

1780

Glossary

adieu (ah-DEW)—the French word for good-bye

brigade (bri-GAYD)—a unit of the army, usually made up of two or more battalions

chamber (CHAYM-buhr)—a bedroom

charmante (SHAR-mont)—a French word for charming

conjecture (con-JEK-sure)—a conclusion you reach by guessing

disposition (diss-puh-ZISH-uhn)—a person's general attitude or temperament

Hessian (he-SHUN)—a German soldier paid by the British to fight the colonists

lackadaisical (la-kuh-DAY-zih-kuhl)—lazy

light horse (LITE HORSS)—a soldier who rode on a horse that weighs less than a draft horse

martial (MAR-shuhl)—warlike and fierce

militia (muh-LISH-uh)—an army composed of ordinary citizens

parlor (PAR-lur)—a formal living room

Quaker (KWAY-kur)—a member of the Religious Society of Friends, a group founded in the 1600s, that prefers simple religious services and opposes war

quarters (KWOR-turs)—housing used by the military

ruminate (ROO-min-ate)—to think deeply about something

sentry (SEN-tree)—a guard

solitude (SAHL-uh-tude)—being alone

Tory (TOR-ee)—an American sympathetic to the British army

vanguard (VAN-gard)—the leading or foremost position of any army advancing into battle

vouchsafe (vowch-SAYF)—to grant something in a gracious manner

Read More

Cheney, Lynne. *When Washington Crossed the Delaware: A Wintertime Story for Young Patriots.* New York: Simon & Schuster Books for Young Readers, 2012.

Forest, Christopher. *The Rebellious Colonists and the Causes of the American Revolution.* The Story of the American Revolution. North Mankato, Minn.: Capstone Press, 2013.

Rajczak, Kristen. *Life During the American Revolution.* What You Didn't Know About History. New York: Gareth Stevens Pub., 2013.

Critical Thinking Using the Common Core

1. Sally and her family were forced to leave their home in Philadelphia during the Revolutionary War. Describe one or two ways this move changed Sally's life. (Key Ideas and Details)

2. General Washington and the Continental Army attacked Hessian soldiers by crossing the Delaware River in 1776. Using the text and what you know about the Revolutionary War, why was this not a typical attack? (Key Details and Ideas)

3. Give three examples from the text that show what life was like for Sally, as a woman in the 1700s. How is this different from the way women are treated today? (Integration of Knowledge and Ideas)

Internet Sites

FactHound offers a safe, fun way to find Internet sites related to this book. All of the sites on FactHound have been researched by our staff.

Here's all you do:

Visit *www.facthound.com*

Type in this code: 9781476541914

 Check out projects, games and lots more at **www.capstonekids.com**

Index